STUDENT BOOK

LET'S GO

LET'S BEGIN 2

5th Edition

Ritsuko Nakata   Karen Frazier   Barbara Hoskins

SONGS AND CHANTS BY
Carolyn Graham

OXFORD
UNIVERSITY PRESS

198 Madison Avenue
New York, NY 10016 USA

Great Clarendon Street, Oxford, OX2 6DP, United Kingdom

Oxford University Press is a department of the University of Oxford. It furthers the University's objective of excellence in research, scholarship, and education by publishing worldwide. Oxford is a registered trade mark of Oxford University Press in the UK and in certain other countries

© Oxford University Press 2018

The moral rights of the author have been asserted

First published in 2018

2023

10 9 8

No unauthorized photocopying

All rights reserved. No part of this publication may be reproduced, stored in a retrieval system, or transmitted, in any form or by any means, without the prior permission in writing of Oxford University Press, or as expressly permitted by law, by licence or under terms agreed with the appropriate reprographics rights organization. Enquiries concerning reproduction outside the scope of the above should be sent to the ELT Rights Department, Oxford University Press, at the address above

You must not circulate this work in any other form and you must impose this same condition on any acquirer

Links to third party websites are provided by Oxford in good faith and for information only. Oxford disclaims any responsibility for the materials contained in any third party website referenced in this work

ISBN: 9780194050081 (STUDENT BOOK)

Printed in China

This book is printed on paper from certified and well-managed sources

ACKNOWLEDGMENTS

Cover illustration: Daniel Griffo

Back cover photograph: Oxford University Press building/David Fisher

Illustrations by: Bernard Adnet: 46, 47; AMS Digital Design: 28, 29; Robin Boyer: 7, 9, 20(1b, 2a), 21, 32, 33, 50, 51, 57, 63(t); Nancy Gayle Carlson: 18, 18, 20(1a); Mircea Catusanu: 8, 16, 42, 52, 60, 61(b), 62, 63(b), 74; Amanda Enright: 56; Mike Gardner: 12(tl), 22(bl), 30(bl), 42(br), 61(br), 67(b), 68(tr), 74(tr); Claudine Gevry: 54, 55; Rick Grayson: 64, 65; Daniel Griffo: 2, 3, 4, 5, 11, 12, 13, 20(b), 22, 23, 30, 31, 40, 41, 48, 49, 58, 59, 66, 65, 67 and cats on pages 1, 4, 6, 8, 10, 12, 14, 16, 19, 20, 22, 24, 26, 28, 30, 32, 34, 37, 38, 40, 42, 44, 46, 48, 50, 52, 55, 56, 58, 60, 62, 64, 66, 68, 70, 72, 74 and 77; Sharon Harmer: 14, 45(b); Bob McMahon: 53; John Kurtz: 17(t), 26, 27, 34, 35, 38, 39, 61(t), 70, 71; John Nez: 15, 25; Jack Pullan: 36, 37, 43(t), 75; Christine Schneider: 6, 17(b), 20(2b), 43(b); Janet Skiles: 72, 73; Mark Stephens: 68, 69; Jim Talbot: 42; Kristin Varner: 44, 45.

Table of Contents

Let's Remember 2

Unit 1   Toys. 4

Unit 2   Colors 12
          Let's Review Units 1 and 2 20

Unit 3   Shapes. 22

Unit 4   Numbers 30
          Let's Review Units 3 and 4 38

Unit 5   Animals 40

Unit 6   Food. 48
          Let's Review Units 5 and 6 56

Unit 7   My Body. 58

Unit 8   I Can 66
          Let's Review Units 7 and 8. 74

Syllabus 76
Word List 78

Kate

Andy

Jenny

Scott

Ginger

Sam

Let's Talk

Let's Learn

Let's Learn More

Let's Learn to Read

Phonics

Let's Review

Let's Remember

A Listen, point, and say. 🔊 1.02

2 Let's Remember

B Listen and say. 🔊 1.03

Hi. I'm Scott.
Hello. I'm Kate.
Hi. I'm Jenny.
Hello. I'm Andy.

C Listen and do. 🔊 1.04

Let's Remember 3

Unit 1 Toys
Let's Talk

A Listen and say. 🔊 1.05

- Hi! What's your name?
- I'm Kate.

B Watch the video.

C Say and act. 🔊 1.06

1. What's your name?
   _____.

2. _____?
   I'm Andy.

3. What's your name?

4 Unit 1 Toys

D Listen, point, and sing.

Hi! What's Your Name?

Hi! What's your name?
I'm Kate.
Hi! What's your name?
I'm Jenny.
Hi! What's your name?
I'm Scott.
Hi! What's your name?
I'm Andy.

Kate, Jenny, Scott, Andy!
Kate, Jenny, Scott, Andy!
Jenny, Andy, Jenny, Andy!
Kate, Jenny, Scott!

E Listen and do.

1. Stand up.

2. Sit down.

I can do this lesson.

Unit 1 Toys 5

Let's Learn

A Learn the words. 🔊 1.09

1. a ball

2. a jump rope

3. a yo-yo

4. a bicycle

B Listen and point. 🔊 1.10

Unit 1 Toys

C Make sentences. 1.11

It's a yo-yo.

D Listen, point, and sing. 1.12

I can do this lesson.

Unit 1 Toys

Let's Learn More

A Learn the words. 1.13

1. a train

2. a car

3. a doll

4. a teddy bear

B Listen and point. 1.14

C Ask and answer.

What is it?

It's a teddy bear.

D Listen, point, and sing.

I can do this lesson.

Let's Learn to Read

Phonics

A Sing and say. 🔊 1.17 🎵

The Alphabet Song

Aa Bb Cc Dd Ee Ff

Gg Hh Ii Jj Kk Ll

Mm Nn Oo Pp Qq Rr

Ss Tt Uu Vv

Ww Xx Yy Zz

B Listen, point, and say. 🔊 1.18

C Listen and point. 🔊 1.19

Andy **J**enny **K**ate **S**cott

D Watch and read along. ▶ 🔊 1.20

I'm Andy.

I'm Jenny.

I'm Kate.

I'm Scott.

I can do this lesson. ☐

Unit 1 Toys

Unit 2 Colors
Let's Talk

A Listen and say. 🔊 1.21

B Watch the video. ▶

C Say and act. 🔊 1.22

1. Hi, boys and girls.
   _____.

2. Goodbye.
   _____.

D Listen and sing.

Hi, Hello, Goodbye

Hi, boys and girls.
　Hello, Miss Jones.
Hi, boys and girls.
　Hello, Miss Jones.
Hi, Andy.
Hello, Jenny.

Goodbye, Kate.
　See you later.
Bye-bye, see you later.
　Bye-bye, see you later.
Bye, Andy.
Goodbye, Jenny.
Goodbye, Kate.
　Bye-bye.

E Listen and do.

1. Come here.

2. Turn around.

I can do this lesson.

Let's Learn

A Learn the words. 🔊 1.25

1. red
2. blue 
3. yellow 
4. green 
5. brown 

B Listen and point. 🔊 1.26

14 Unit 2 Colors

C Make sentences. 🔊 1.27

"It's blue."

D Listen and point. 🔊 1.28

I can do this lesson.

Unit 2 Colors 15

Let's Learn More

A **Learn the words.** 🔊 1.29

1. purple
2. orange
3. black
4. white
5. pink

B **Listen and point.** 🔊 1.30

16 Unit 2 Colors

C Ask and answer. 🔊 1.31

What color is it?

It's purple.

D Listen, point, and chant. 🔊 1.32 ♪♪

I can do this lesson.

Unit 2 Colors 17

Let's Learn to Read

Phonics

A Sing and say. 🔊 1.33

A B C D E F G H I J K L M N O P Q R S T U V W X Y Z
a b c d e f g h i j k l m n o p q r s t u v w x y z

B Listen, point, and say. 🔊 1.34

Aa
apple  ant

Bb
ball  bird

Cc
cat  car

Dd
dog  doll

18 Unit 2 Colors

C Watch, point, and chant.

The ABCD Chant

A a apple    ant 
B b ball    bird 
C c cat    car 
D d dog    doll

D Find the letters. Name the pictures.

"What is it?"

"It's a ball."

E Listen and read along.

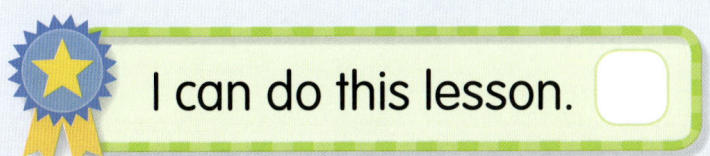
I can do this lesson.

Unit 2 Colors

Let's Review

A Listen and circle. 🔊 1.37

1.

a.   b.

2.

a.   b.

3.

a.   b.

4.

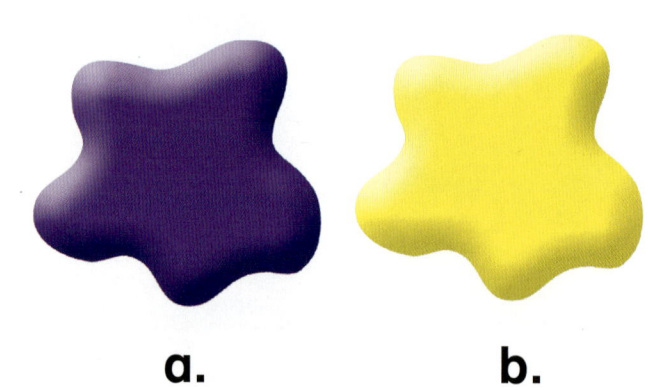

a.   b.

5.

a.   b.

6.

a.   b.

20 Units 1 and 2 Review

School Supplies

A Say these. 🔊 1.38

1. paper 2. scissors 3. glue 4. paint 5. tape

I have paper.

I can talk about Unit 1.

1. What's your name?
2. What is it?

I can talk about Unit 2.

1. Say Hello. Goodbye.
2. What color is it?

Unit 3 Shapes

Let's Talk

A Listen and say. 🔊 1.39

How are you today?

I'm fine, thank you.

B Watch the video. ▶

C Say and act. 🔊 1.40

1. How are you today?
   _____.

2. _____?
   I'm fine, thank you.

D Listen and sing.

How Are You Today?

How are you today?
 I'm fine, thank you.
How are you?
 I'm fine, thank you.
How are you today?
 I'm fine, thank you.
How are you?
 I'm fine.

E Listen and do.

1. Walk.

2. Run.

I can do this lesson.

Unit 3 Shapes

Let's Learn

A Learn the words. 🔊 1.43

1. a circle

2. a square

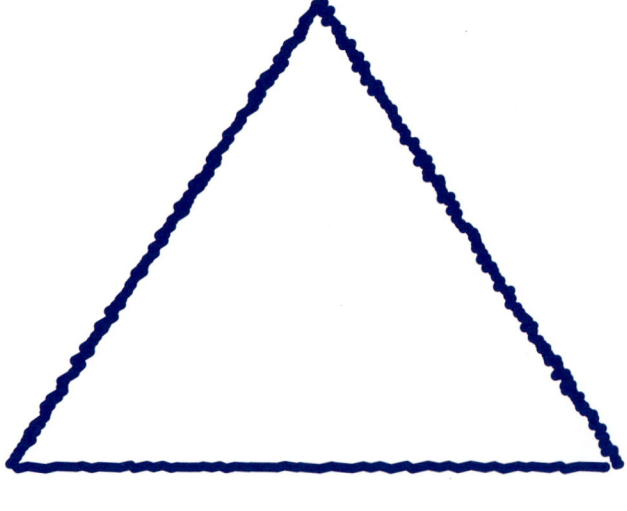

3. a triangle

4. a heart

B Listen and point. 🔊 1.44

C Make sentences. 🔊 1.45

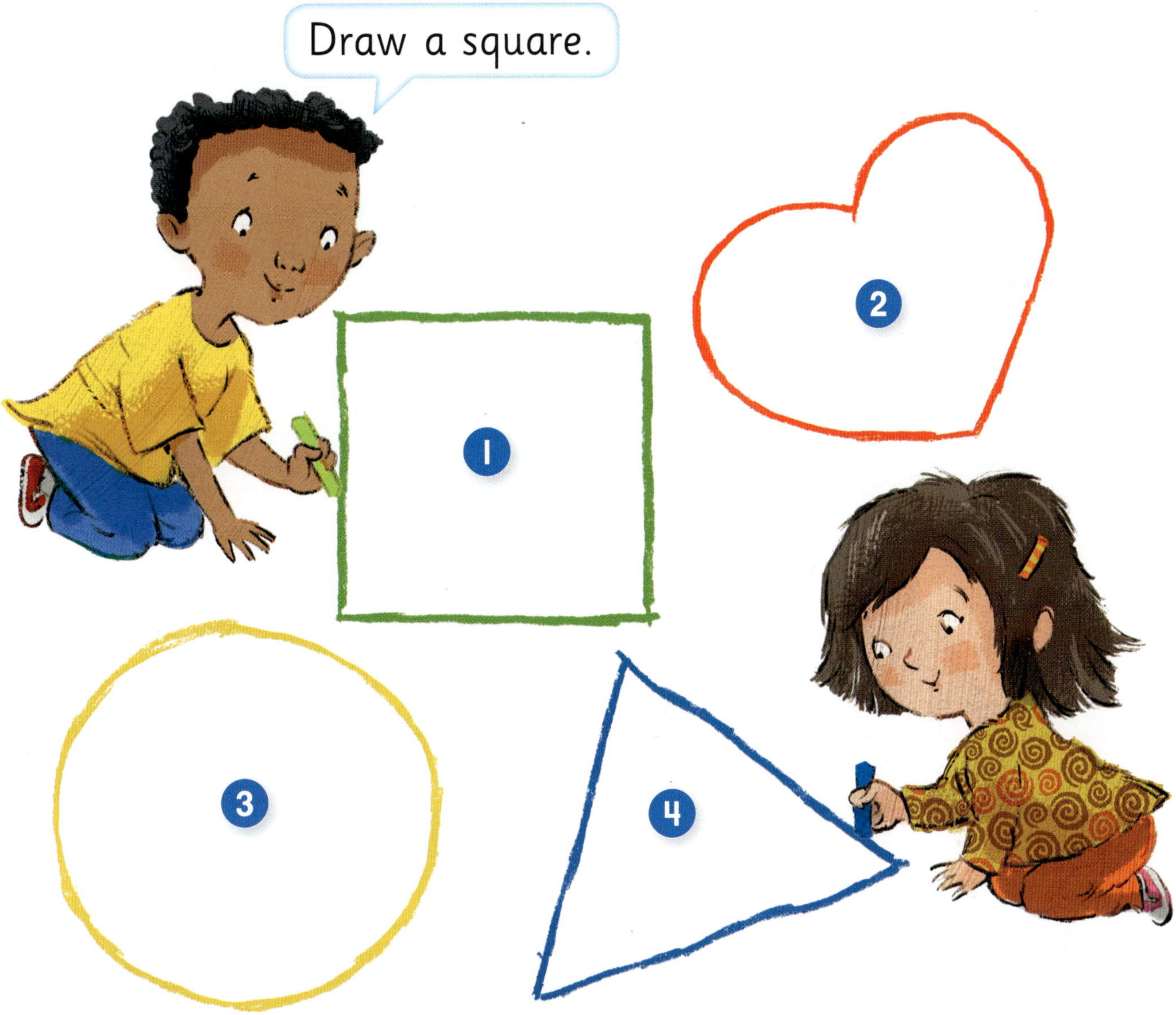

"Draw a square."

1. (square)
2. (heart)
3. (circle)
4. (triangle)

D Listen, point, and chant. 🔊 1.46 🎵

I can do this lesson.

Unit 3 Shapes 25

Let's Learn More

A Learn the words. 1.47

1. a star

2. a rectangle

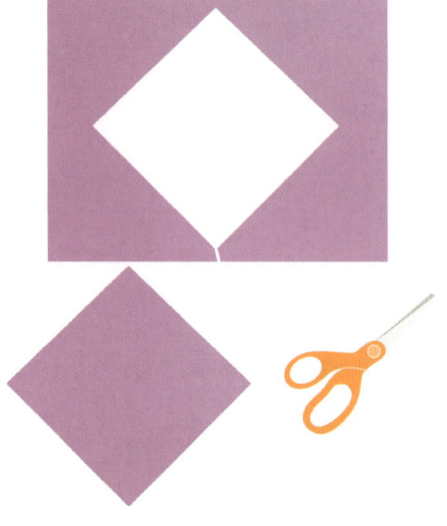

3. a diamond

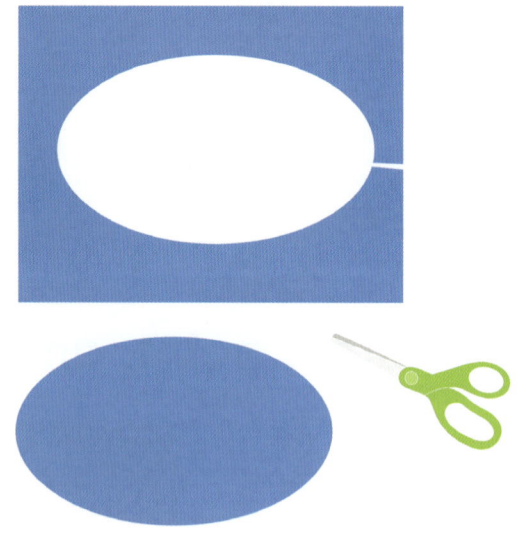

4. an oval

B Listen and point. 1.48

C Ask and answer. 🔊 1.49

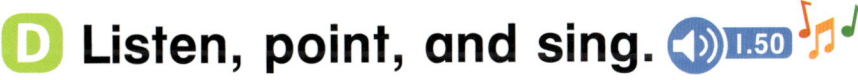

Is it a star?
Yes, it is.

Is it a rectangle?
No, it isn't. It's a diamond.

D Listen, point, and sing. 🔊 1.50 🎵

I can do this lesson.

Let's Learn to Read

Phonics

A Sing and say. 🔊 1.51 🎵

A B C D **E F G H** I J K L M N O P Q R S T U V W X Y Z
a b c d **e f g h** i j k l m n o p q r s t u v w x y z

B Listen, point, and say. 🔊 1.52

Ee

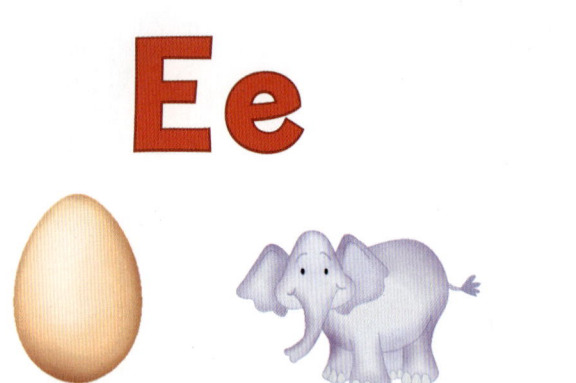

egg   elephant

Ff

fish   farm

Gg

gorilla   goat

Hh

heart   house

28 Unit 3 Shapes

C Watch, point, and chant.

The EFGH Chant

E e egg  elephant
F f fish  farm 
G g goat  gorilla 
H h house  heart

D Find the letters. Name the pictures.

Is it a heart?

Yes, it is.

E Listen and read along.

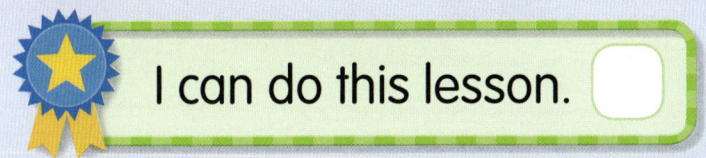

Unit 4 Numbers
Let's Talk

A Listen and say. 1.55

May I come in?

Sure! Please come in!

B Watch the video.

C Say and act. 1.56

1. May I come in?

   _____!

2. _____?

   Sure! Please come in!

D Listen and sing. 🔊 1.57 🎵

May I Come In?

May I come in?
  Sure! Please come in!
  Please come in!
May I come in?
May I come in?
  Sure! Please come in!

E Listen and do. 🔊 1.58

1. Go.

2. Stop.

I can do this lesson.

Let's Learn

A Learn the numbers. 🔊 1.59

1

3

2

4

5

B Listen and point. 🔊 1.60

32 Unit 4 Numbers

C Make sentences. 🔊 1.61

D Listen, point, and sing. 🔊 1.62 🎵

1 2 3 4 5

I can do this lesson.

Unit 4 Numbers 33

Let's Learn More

A Learn the numbers. 🔊 1.63

6

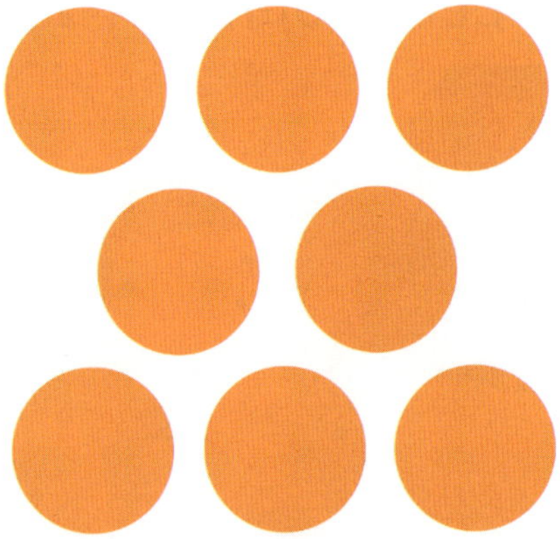

7

8

9

10

B Listen and point. 🔊 1.64

C Ask and answer. 🔊 1.65

How many?

D Listen, point, and sing. 🔊 1.66 🎵

Unit 4 Numbers 35

Let's Learn to Read

Phonics

A Sing and say. 🔊 1.67 ♪

A B C D E F G H **I J K L** M N O P Q R S T U V W X Y Z

a b c d e f g h **i j k l** m n o p q r s t u v w x y z

B Listen, point, and say. 🔊 1.68

Ii

igloo

iguana

Jj

jump rope

jeans

Kk

kangaroo

kite

Ll

lion

ladybug

C Watch, point, and chant.

The IJKL Chant

I i igloo    iguana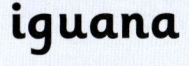

J j jump rope    jeans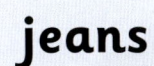

K k kite    kangaroo

L l ladybug  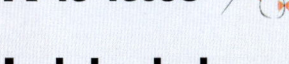   lion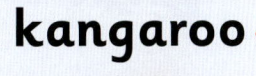

D Find the letters. Name the pictures.

"Is it a lion?" "Yes, it is."

E Listen and read along.

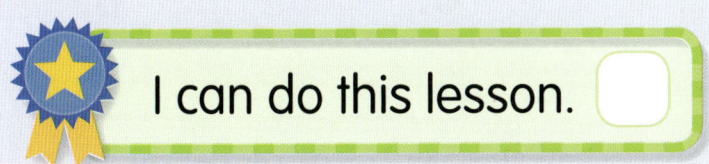

I can do this lesson.

Unit 4 Numbers 37

Let's Review

A Listen and circle. 🔊 1.71

1.

a.   b.

2.

a.   b.

3.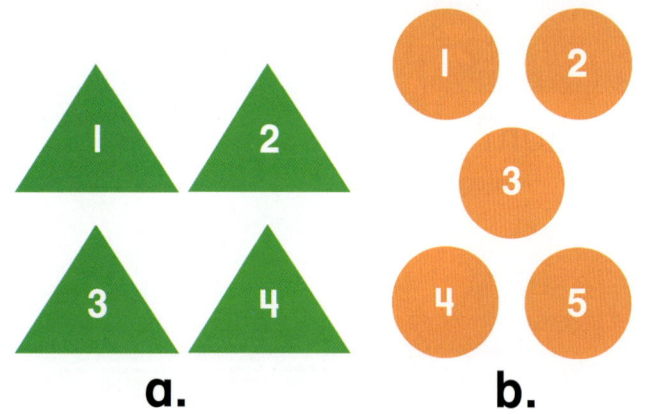

a.   b.

4.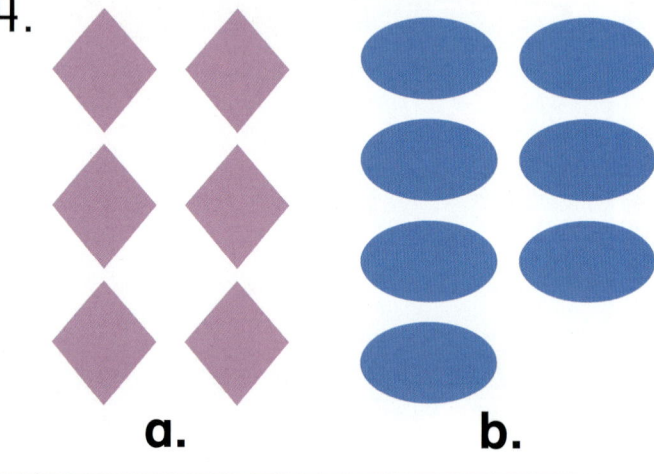

a.   b.

5.

a.   b.

6.

a.   b.

Classroom Commands

A Say these. 🔊 1.72

1. Take out your pencil.
2. Put away your pencil.
3. Open your book.
4. Close your book.

Please take out your pencil.

I can talk about Unit 3.

1. How are you today?
2. Is it a diamond?

I can talk about Unit 4.

1. Let's count.
2. How many?

Speaking Bonus 39

Unit 5 Animals
Let's Talk

A Listen and say. 🔊 2.02

Here you are.

Thank you.

B Watch the video. ▶

C Say and act. 🔊 2.03

1.

   Here you are.

   _____.

2.

   _____.

   Thank you.

D Listen and sing. 🔊 2.04 🎵

Here You Are. Thank You!

Here you are.
  Thank you, thank you!
Here you are.
  Thank you!
Here you are.
  Thank you, thank you!
Here you are.
  Thank you!

E Listen and do. 🔊 2.05

1. Jump.

2. Skip.

 I can do this lesson. ☐

Unit 5 Animals   41

Let's Learn

A Learn the words. 🔊 2.06

1. dog

2. dogs

3. cat

4. cats

5. bird

6. birds

B Listen and point. 🔊 2.07

C Make sentences. 🔊 2.08

"Let's count the cats."

"1 cat, 2 cats."

D Listen, point, and sing. 🔊 2.09 🎵

I can do this lesson.

Unit 5 Animals 43

Let's Learn More

A Learn the words. 🔊 2.10

1. cow
2. cows
3. rabbit
4. rabbits
5. duck
6. ducks

B Listen and point. 🔊 2.11

Unit 5 Animals

C Ask and answer. 🔊 2.12

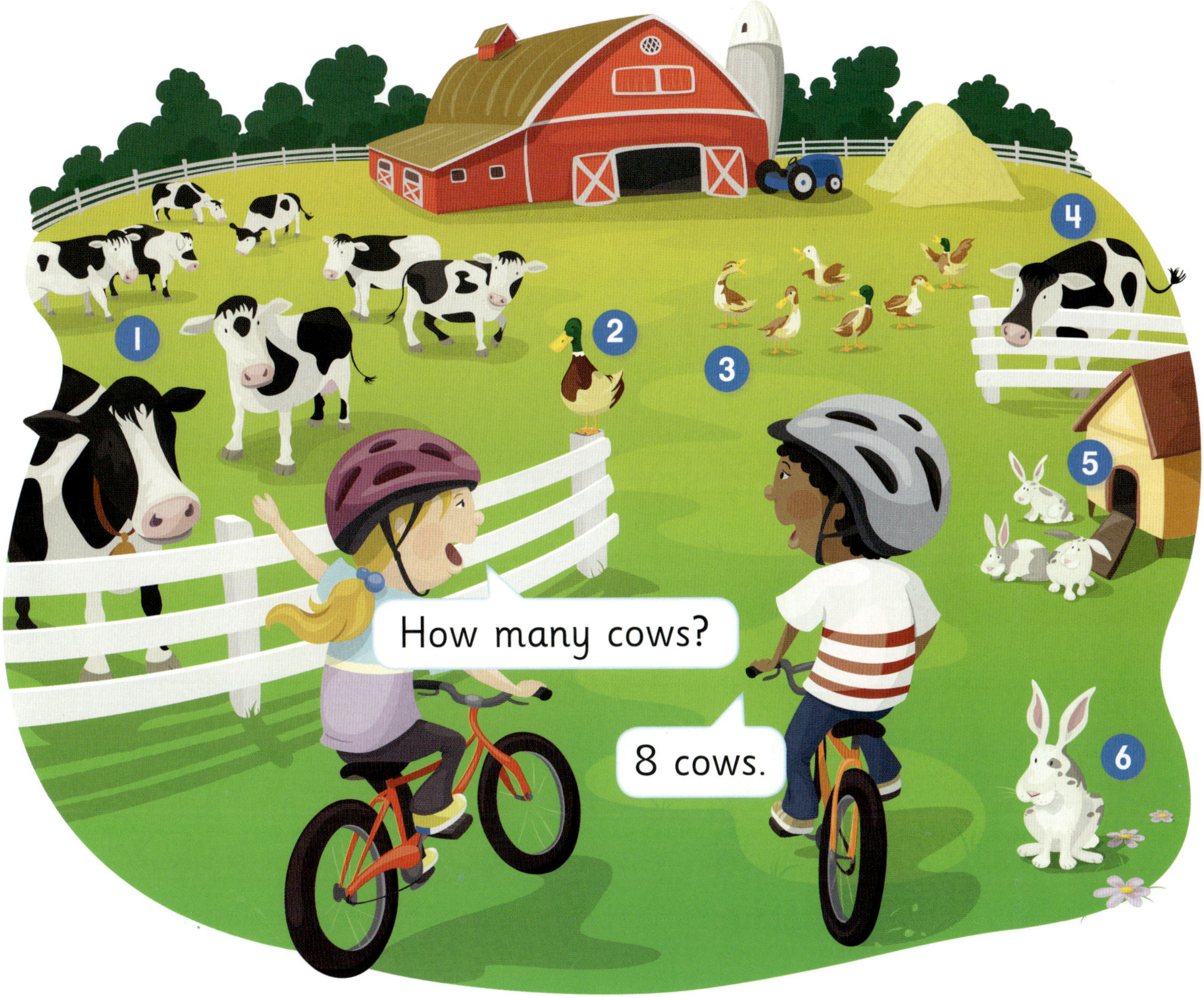

How many cows?

8 cows.

D Listen, point, and sing. 🔊 2.13 🎵

I can do this lesson.

Unit 5 Animals 45

Let's Learn to Read

Phonics

A Sing and say. 🔊 2.14 🎵

A B C D E F G H I J K L **M N O P** Q R S T U V W X Y Z
a b c d e f g h i j k l **m n o p** q r s t u v w x y z

B Listen, point, and say. 🔊 2.15

Mm

moon   monkey

Nn

nest   net

Oo

octopus   ostrich

Pp

panda   popcorn

C Watch, point, and chant.

The MNOP Chant

M m monkey   moon
N n nest   net
O o ostrich   octopus
P p panda   popcorn

D Find the letters. Name the pictures.

"How many eggs?" "1 egg."

E Listen and read along.

I can do this lesson.

Unit 5 Animals

Unit 6 Food
Let's Talk

A Listen and say. 🔊 2.18

B Watch the video.

C Say and act. 🔊 2.19

1. How old are you?

_____.

2. _____? I'm 10.

D Listen and sing. 2.20

How Old Are You?

How old are you?
I'm 6.
How old are you?
I'm 7.
1, 2, 3, 4, 5, 6, 7!
How old are you?
I'm 5.
How old are you?
I'm 10.
1, 2, 3, 4, 5, 6, 7, 8, 9, 10!

E Listen and do. 2.21

1. Make a line.

2. Make a circle.

I can do this lesson.

Unit 6 Food

Let's Learn

A Learn the words. 🔊 2.22

1. ice cream

2. pizza

3. cake

4. chicken

B Listen and point. 🔊 2.23

C Make sentences. 🔊 2.24

I like cake.

D Listen, point, and sing. 🔊 2.25 🎵

   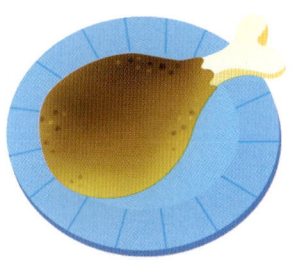

I can do this lesson.

Unit 6 Food 51

Let's Learn More

A Learn the words. 🔊 2.26

1. milk

2. fish

3. bread

4. rice

B Listen, point, and chant. 🔊 2.27 ♪♪

52 Unit 6 Food

C Ask and answer. 🔊 2.28

1.
2.
3.
4.
5.
6.

D What about you?

Do you like fish?

 I can do this lesson.

Let's Learn to Read

Phonics

A Sing and say. 🔊 2.29

A B C D E F G H I J K L M N O P **Q R S T** U V W X Y Z
a b c d e f g h i j k l m n o p **q r s t** u v w x y z

B Listen, point, and say. 🔊 2.30

queen   quilt   rabbit   rock

sun   sandwich   tiger   teapot

C Watch, point, and chant.

The QRST Chant

Q q queen  quilt

R r rabbit rock

S s sun  sandwich

T t tiger  teapot

D Find the letters. Name the pictures.

Do you like cake? Yes, I do.

E Listen and read along.

 I can do this lesson.

Unit 6 Food 55

Let's Review

A Listen and circle. 🔊 2.33

1.
   a.   b.

2.
   a.   b.

3.
   a.   b.

4.
   a.   b.

5.
   a.   b.

6.
   a.   b.

56 Units 5 and 6 Review

The Weather

A Say these. 🔊 2.34

1. sunny

2. cloudy

3. windy

4. rainy

5. snowy

It's sunny.

I can talk about Unit 5.

1. Say and act.
   Here you are. Thank you.

2. How many cows?

I can talk about Unit 6.

1. How old are you?

2. Do you like pizza?

Speaking Bonus

Unit 7 My Body

Let's Talk

A Listen and say. 🔊 2.35

Oops! I'm sorry.

That's OK.

B Watch the video. ▶

C Say and act. 🔊 2.36

1. Oops! I'm sorry.

   _____.

2. _____.

   That's OK.

D Listen and sing. 🔊 2.37 🎵

Oops! I'm Sorry

Oops! I'm sorry.
That's OK.
Oops! I'm sorry.
Oops! I'm sorry.

Oops! I'm sorry.
That's OK.
Oops! I'm sorry.
That's OK.

E Listen and do. 🔊 2.38

1. Stamp your feet.

2. Clap your hands.

I can do this lesson.

Let's Learn

A Learn the words. 🔊 2.39

1. head

2. shoulders

3. knees

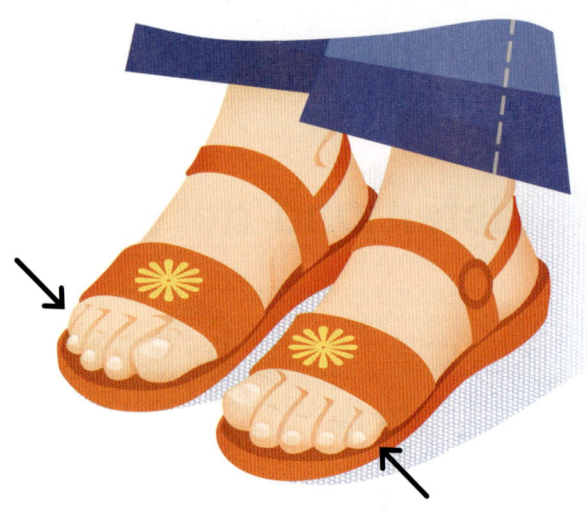

4. toes

B Listen and point. 🔊 2.40

C Make sentences. 🔊 2.41

"I can touch my head."

1.
2.
3.
4.

D Listen, point, and chant. 🔊 2.42 ♪♪

I can do this lesson.

Unit 7 My Body 61

Let's Learn More

A Learn the words. 🔊 2.43

1. eyes

2. ears

3. mouth

4. nose

B Listen and point. 🔊 2.44

62 Unit 7 My Body

C Ask and answer. 2.45

"What can you do?" "I can touch my eyes."

D Listen, point, and sing. 2.46

I can do this lesson.

Unit 7 My Body

Let's Learn to Read

Phonics

A Sing and say. 🔊 2.47

A B C D E F G H I J K L M N O P Q R S T **U V W** X Y Z
a b c d e f g h i j k l m n o p q r s t **u v w** x y z

B Listen, point, and say. 🔊 2.48

umbrella   up   violin   vest

watch   water

64 Unit 7 My Body

C Watch, point, and chant. 🔊 2.49

The UVW Chant

U u up    umbrella

V v vest    violin

W w water    watch

D Find the letters. Name the pictures.

What can you do?

I can touch my nose.

E Listen and read along. 🔊 2.50

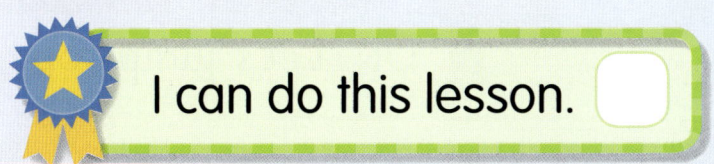

I can do this lesson.

Unit 8 I Can

Let's Talk

A Listen and say.

Let's play.

OK. Let's play ball.

OK. Let's play tag.

OK. Let's jump rope.

B Watch the video.

C Say and act.

1. Let's play.
   _____.

2. _____.
   OK. Let's jump rope.

D Listen and sing. 2.53

Let's Play

Let's play.
OK!
Let's play.
OK, OK!
Let's play, let's play.
OK, let's play!

Let's play tag.
OK, let's play, let's play!
Let's jump rope.
OK, OK, let's play!
Let's play ball.
OK, let's play, let's play!
Hey, let's play, let's play.
OK!

E Listen and do. 2.54

1. Point to the board.

2. Go to the board.

I can do this lesson.

Unit 8 I Can 67

Let's Learn

A Learn the words. 🔊 2.55

1. ride a bicycle

2. sing a song

3. fly a kite

4. bounce a ball

B Listen and point. 🔊 2.56

68 Unit 8 I Can

C Make sentences. 🔊 2.57

D Listen, point, and chant. 🔊 2.58 🎵

I can do this lesson.

Let's Learn More

A Learn the words. 🔊 2.59

1. swim

2. smile

3. wink

4. dance

B Listen and point. 🔊 2.60

70 Unit 8 I Can

C Ask and answer. 🔊 2.61

"Can you dance?" "Yes, I can."

"Can you dance?" "No, I can't."

D Listen and chant. 🔊 2.62

I can do this lesson.

Let's Learn to Read

Phonics

A Sing and say. 🔊 2.63 🎵

A B C D E F G H I J K L M N O P Q R S T U V W **X Y Z**

a b c d e f g h i j k l m n o p q r s t u v w **x y z**

B Listen, point, and say. 🔊 2.64

fox   box   yarn   yak

zebra   zero

72 Unit 8 I Can

C Watch, point, and chant.

The XYZ Chant

X x fox  box

Y y yarn  yak

Z z zebra  zero 0

D Find the letters. Name the pictures.

"I can't dance."

"I can dance."

E Listen and read along.

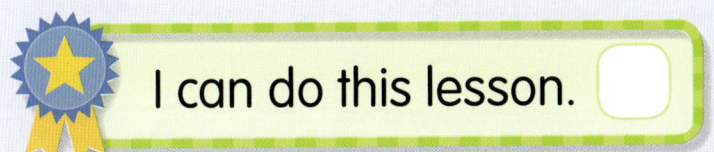

I can do this lesson.

Let's Review

A Listen and circle. 🔊 2.67

1.

a.   b.

2.

a.   b.

3.

a.   b.

4.

a.   b.

5.

a.   b.

6.

a.   b.

Units 7 and 8 Review

Days of the Week

A Say these. 🔊 2.68

It's Sunday.

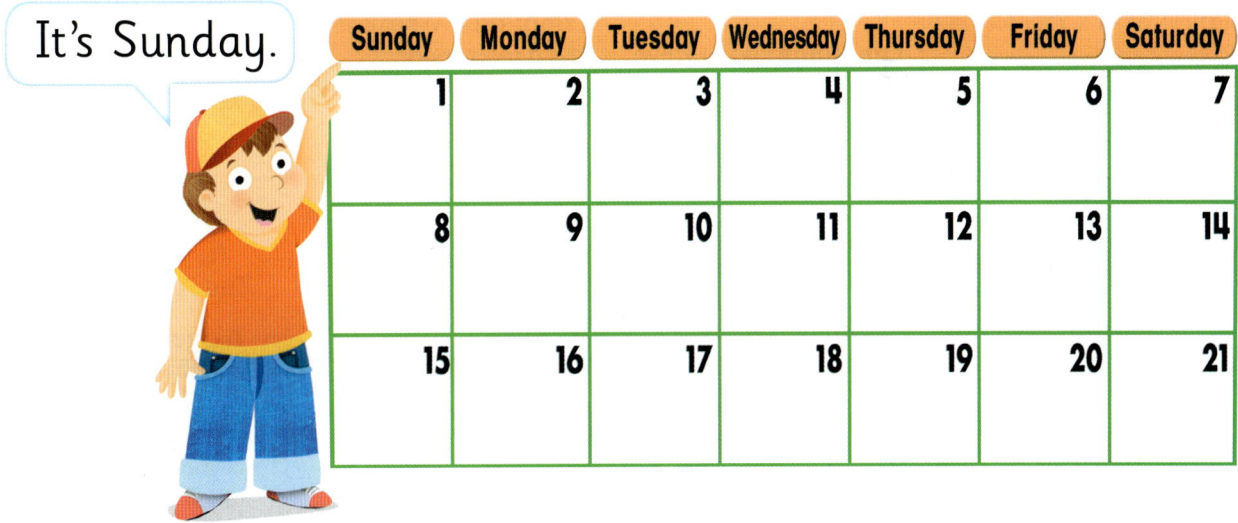

B Listen, point, and sing. 🔊 2.69 🎵

I can talk about Unit 7.

1. I can touch my ears.
2. What can you do?

I can talk about Unit 8.

1. I can fly a kite.
2. Can you dance?

Speaking Bonus

Let's Begin 2 Syllabus

Let's Remember
Alphabet Aa–Zz   **Language:** Hi. I'm Scott. Hello. I'm Kate. Touch your shoulders. Touch your elbows. Touch your knees. Touch your feet.

Let's Talk	Let's Learn	Let's Learn More	Let's Learn to Read
Unit 1 Toys			
Conversation: Hi, what's your name? I'm Kate. **Song:** Hi! What's Your Name? **Listen and do:** Stand up. Sit down.	**Toys:** a ball, a jump rope, a yo-yo, a bicycle **Language:** It's a yo-yo.	**Toys:** a train, a car, a doll, a teddy bear **Language:** What is it? It's a teddy bear.	**Phonics** The Alphabet Song Aa–Zz **Find the letters:** Andy, Jenny, Kate, Scott
Unit 2 Colors			
Conversation: Hi, boys and girls. Hello, Miss Jones. Goodbye. See you later. **Song:** Hi, Hello, Goodbye **Listen and do:** Come here. Turn around.	**Colors:** red, blue, yellow, green, brown **Language:** It's blue.	**Colors:** purple, orange, black, white, pink **Language:** What color is it? It's purple.	**Phonics** The Alphabet Song Aa–Zz **Alphabet A–D:** apple, ant, ball, bird, cat, car, dog, doll **The ABCD Chant** **Sentences:** What is it? It's a ball.
Let's Review Units 1 and 2			**Speaking Bonus**
Unit 3 Shapes			
Conversation: How are you today? I'm fine, thank you. **Song:** How Are You Today? **Listen and do:** Walk. Run.	**Shapes:** a circle, a square, a triangle, a heart **Language:** Draw a square.	**Shapes:** a star, a rectangle, a diamond, an oval **Language:** Is it a star? Yes, it is. Is it a rectangle? No, it isn't. It's a diamond.	**Phonics** The Alphabet Song Aa–Zz **Alphabet E–H:** egg, elephant, fish, farm, gorilla, goat, heart, house **The EFGH Chant** **Sentences:** Is it a heart? Yes, it is.
Unit 4 Numbers			
Conversation: May I come in? Sure! Please come in! **Song:** May I Come In? **Listen and do:** Go. Stop.	**Numbers 1–5:** 1, 2, 3, 4, 5 **Language:** Let's count. 1, 2, 3, 4...5!	**Numbers 6–10:** 6, 7, 8, 9, 10 **Language:** How many? 7.	**Phonics** The Alphabet Song Aa–Zz **Alphabet I–L:** igloo, iguana, jump rope, jeans, kangaroo, kite, lion, ladybug **The IJKL Chant** **Sentences:** Is it a lion? Yes, it is.
Let's Review Units 3 and 4			**Speaking Bonus**

Let's Talk	Let's Learn	Let's Learn More	Let's Learn to Read
Unit 5 Animals			
Conversation: Here you are. Thank you. **Song:** Here You Are. Thank You! **Listen and do:** Jump. Skip.	**Pets:** dog, dogs, cat, cats, bird, birds **Language:** Let's count the cats. 1 cat, 2 cats.	**Farm Animals:** cow, cows, rabbit, rabbits, duck, ducks **Language:** How many cows? 8 cows.	**Phonics** The Alphabet Song Aa–Zz **Alphabet M–P:** moon, monkey, nest, net, octopus, ostrich, panda, popcorn The MNOP Chant **Sentences:** How many eggs? 1 egg.
Unit 6 Food			
Conversation: How old are you? I'm 6. **Song:** How Old Are You? **Listen and do:** Make a line. Make a circle.	**Food:** ice cream, pizza, cake, chicken **Language:** I like cake.	**Food:** milk, fish, bread, rice **Language:** Do you like fish? Yes, I do. No, I don't.	**Phonics** The Alphabet Song Aa–Zz **Alphabet Q–T:** queen, quilt, rabbit, rock, sun, sandwich, tiger, teapot The QRST Chant **Sentences:** Do you like cake? Yes, I do.
Let's Review Units 5 and 6			**Speaking Bonus**
Unit 7 My Body			
Conversation: Oops! I'm sorry! That's OK. **Song:** Oops! I'm Sorry **Listen and do:** Stamp your feet. Clap your hands.	**Body:** head, shoulders, knees, toes **Language:** I can touch my head.	**Face:** eyes, ears, mouth, nose **Language:** What can you do? I can touch my eyes.	**Phonics** The Alphabet Song Aa–Zz **Alphabet U–W:** umbrella, up, violin, vest, watch, water The UVW Chant **Sentences:** What can you do? I can touch my nose.
Unit 8 I Can			
Conversation: Let's play. OK. Let's play ball. OK. Let's play tag. OK. Let's jump rope. **Song:** Let's Play **Listen and do:** Point to the board. Go to the board.	**Activities:** ride a bicycle, sing a song, fly a kite, bounce a ball **Language:** I can fly a kite. I can't fly a kite.	**Activities:** swim, smile, wink, dance **Language:** Can you dance? Yes, I can. No, I can't.	**Phonics** The Alphabet Song Aa–Zz **Alphabet X–Z:** fox, box, yarn, yak, zebra, zero The XYZ Chant **Sentences:** I can dance. I can't dance.
Let's Review Units 7 and 8			**Speaking Bonus**

Let's Begin 2 Syllabus

Word List

A
a 6
an 26
and 12
ant 18
apple 18
are 22

B
ball 6
bicycle 6
bird 18
birds 42
black 16
blue 14
board 67
book 39
bounce 68
box 72
boys 12
bread 52
brown 14

C
cake 50
can 61
can't 69
car 8
cat 18
cats 42
chicken 50
circle 24
clap 59
close 39
cloudy 57
color 17
come here . . . 13
come in 30
count 33
cow 44
cows 44

D
dance 70
diamond 26
do 53
dog 18
dogs 42
doll 8
don't 53
draw 25
duck 44
ducks 44

E
ears 62
egg 28
eggs 47
eight (8) 34
elephant 28
eyes 62

F
farm 28
feet 59
fine 22
fish 28
five (5) 32
fly 68
four (4) 32
fox 72
Friday 75

G
girls 12
glue 21
go 31
goat 28
goodbye 12
gorilla 28
green 14

H
hands 59
have 21
head 60
heart 24
hello 12
here 40
hi 3
house 28
how 22

I
I 21
I'm 3
I'm sorry . . . 58
ice cream . . . 50
igloo 36
iguana 36
is 9
isn't 27
it 9
it's 7

J
jeans 36
jump 41
jump rope . . . 6

K
kangaroo 36
kite 36
knees 60

L
ladybug 36
later 14
let's 33
like 51
line 49
lion 36

M
make 49
may 30
milk 52
miss 12
Monday 75
monkey 46
moon 46
mouth 62
my 61

N
name 4
nest 46
net 46
nine (9) 34
no 27
nose 62

O
octopus 46
old 48
one (1) 32
oops 58
open 39
orange 16
ostrich 46
oval 26

P
paint 21
panda 46
paper 21
pencil 39
pink 16
pizza 50
play 66
please 30
point 67
popcorn 46
purple 16
put away 39

Q
queen 54
quilt 54

R
rabbit 44
rabbits 44
rainy 57
rectangle 26
red 14
rice 52
ride 68
rock 54
run 23

S
sandwich 54
Saturday 75
scissors 21
see you
  later 12
seven (7) 34
shoulders 60
sing 68
sit down 5
six (6) 34
skip 41
smile 70
snowy 57
song 68
square 24
stamp 59
stand up 5
star 26
stop 31
sun 54
Sunday 75
sunny 57
sure 30
swim 70

T
tag 66
take out 39
tape 21
teapot 54
teddy bear . . . 8
ten (10) 34
thank you . . . 22
that's OK . . . 58
the 43
three (3) 32
Thursday 75
tiger 54
to 67

today 22
toes 60
touch 61
train 8
triangle 24
Tuesday 75
turn around . . 13
two (2) 32

U
umbrella 64
up 64

V
vest 64
violin 64

W
walk 23
watch 64
water 64
Wednesday . . 75
what 9
what's 4
white 16
windy 57
wink 70

Y
yak 72
yarn 72
yellow 14
yes 27
yo-yo 6
you 12
your 4

Z
zebra 72
zero (0) 72

78   Let's Begin 2 Word List